Mindful
Mandalas

Copyright: Published in the United States by Peter Raymond
Published July 2018
ISBN-13: 978-1722291297
ISBN-10: 172229129X

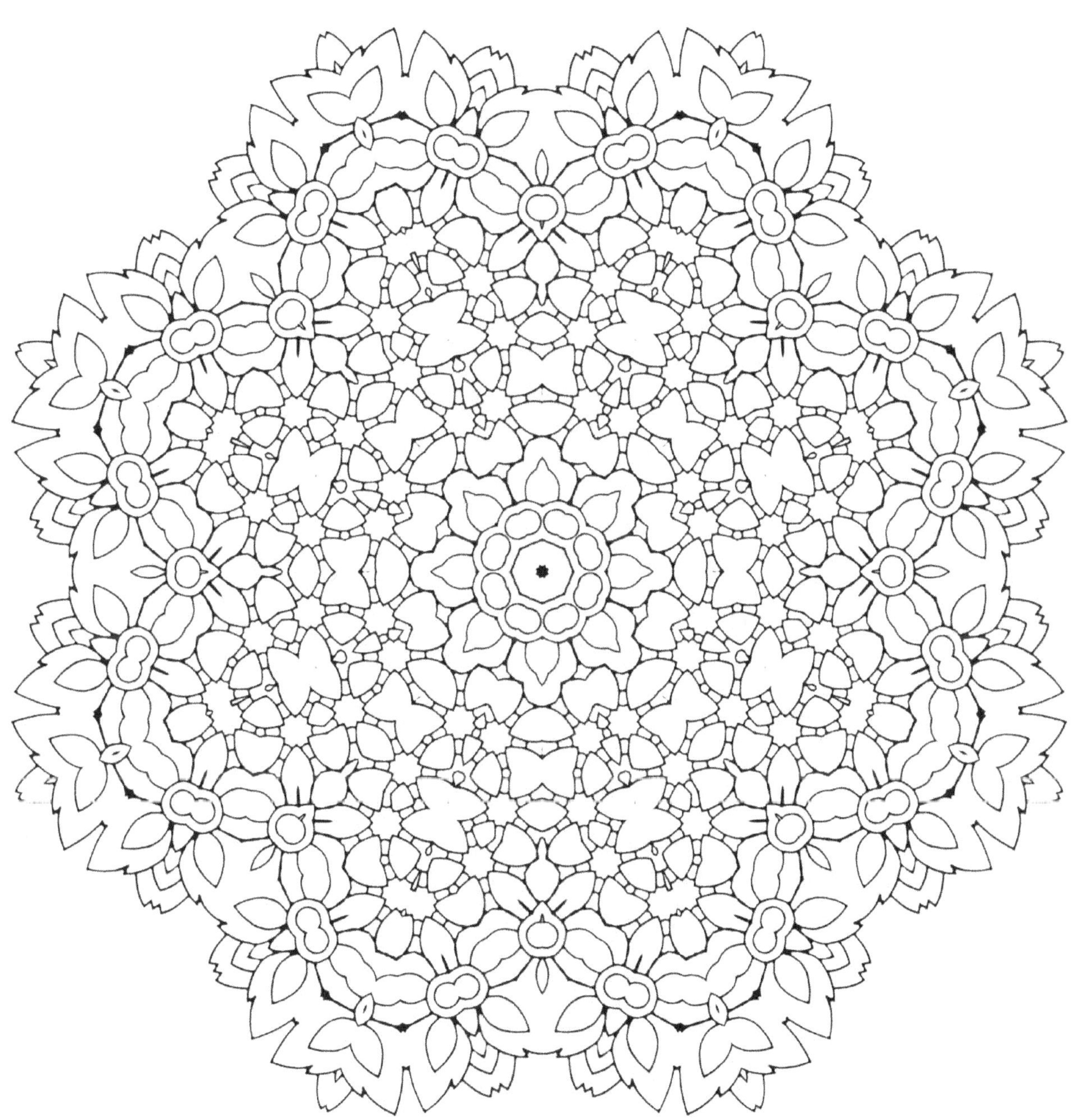

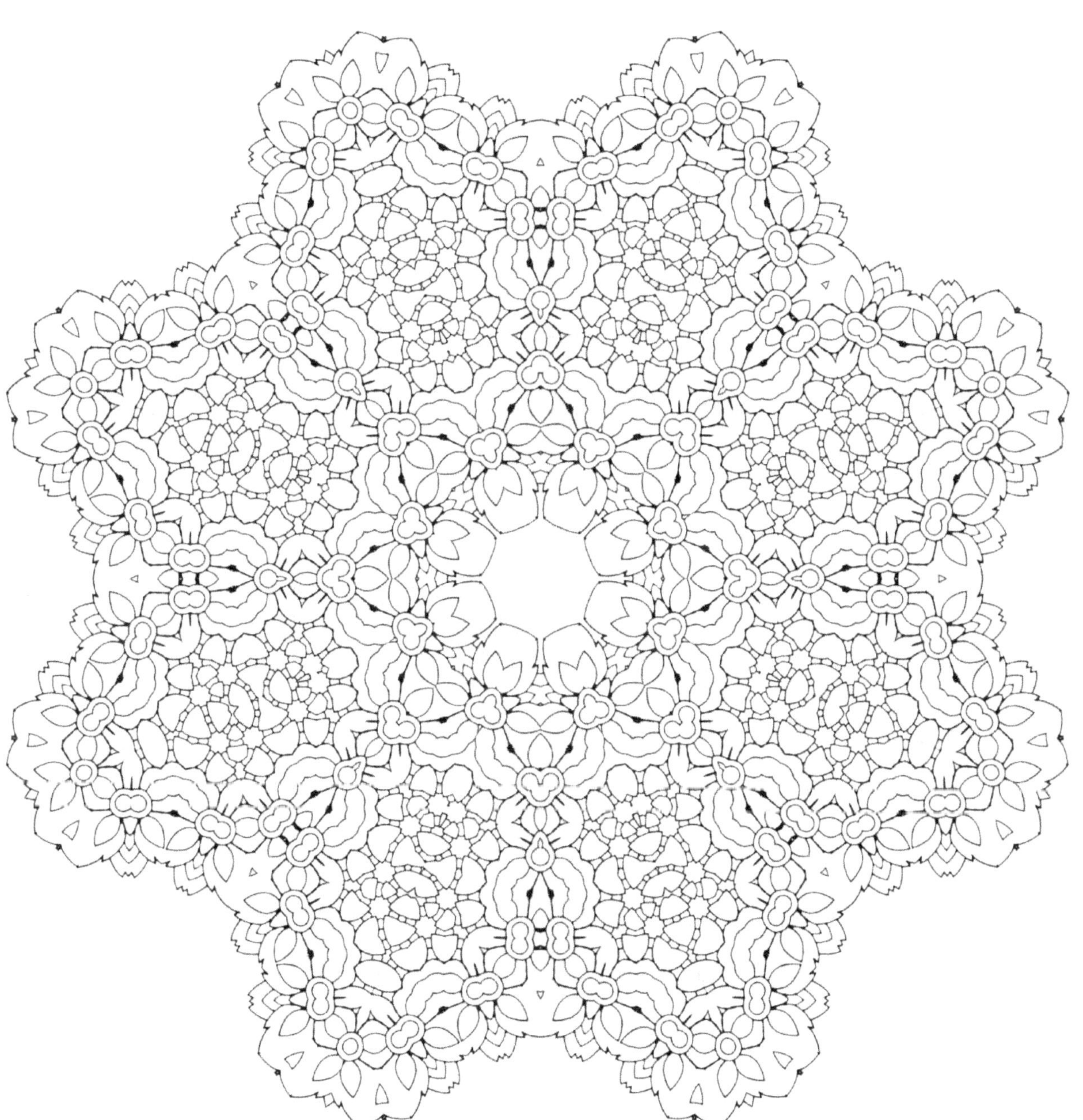

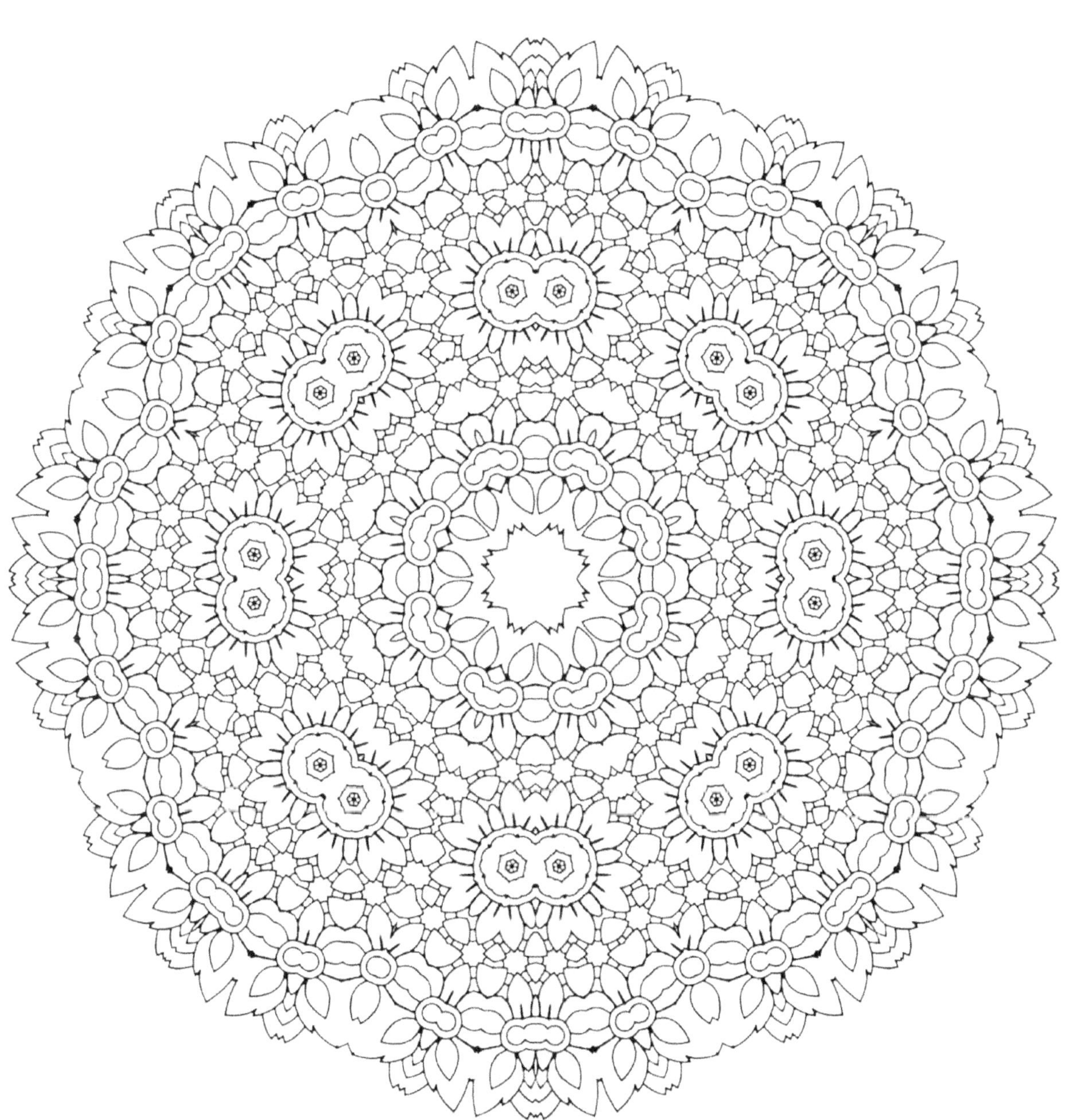

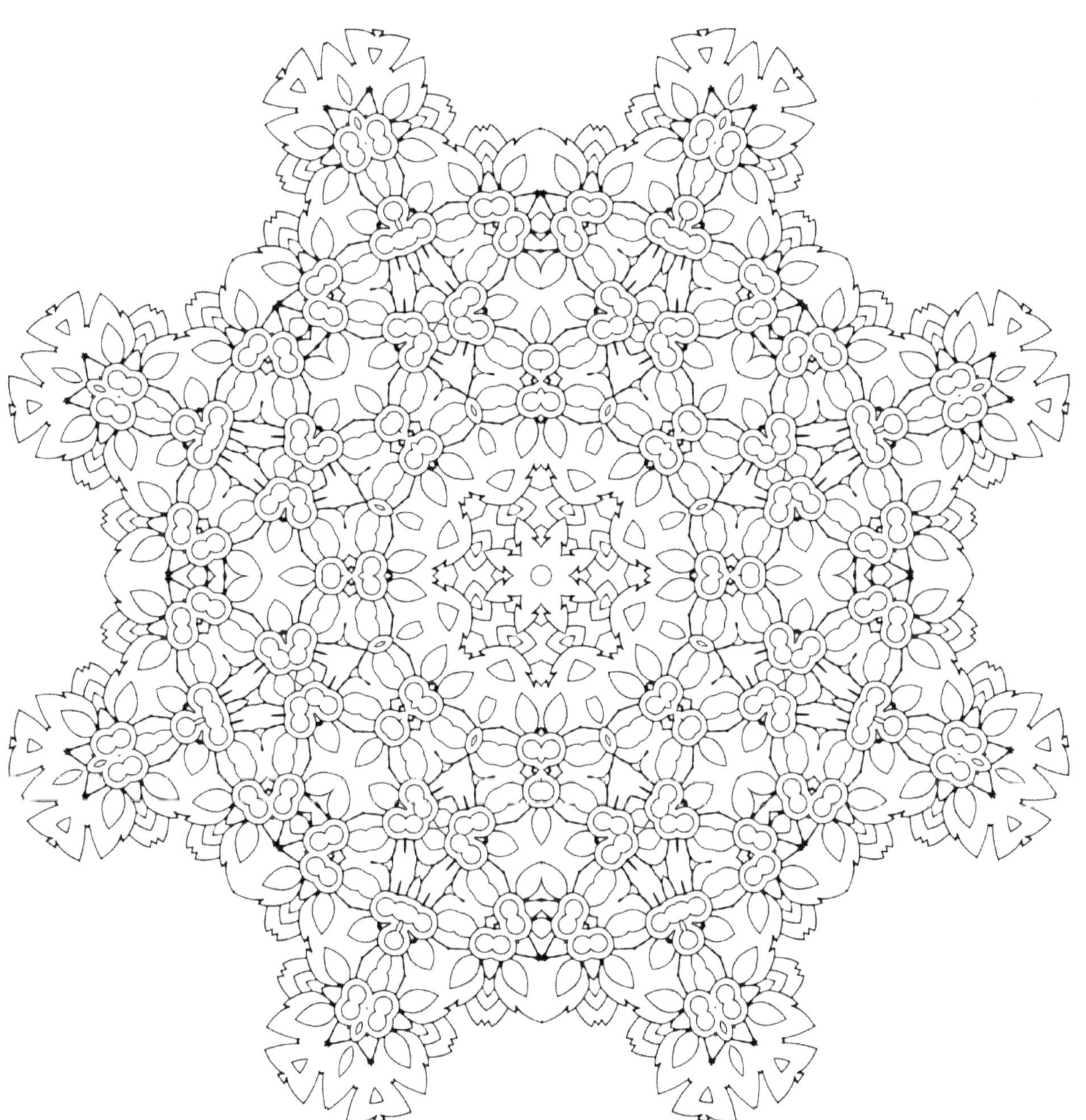

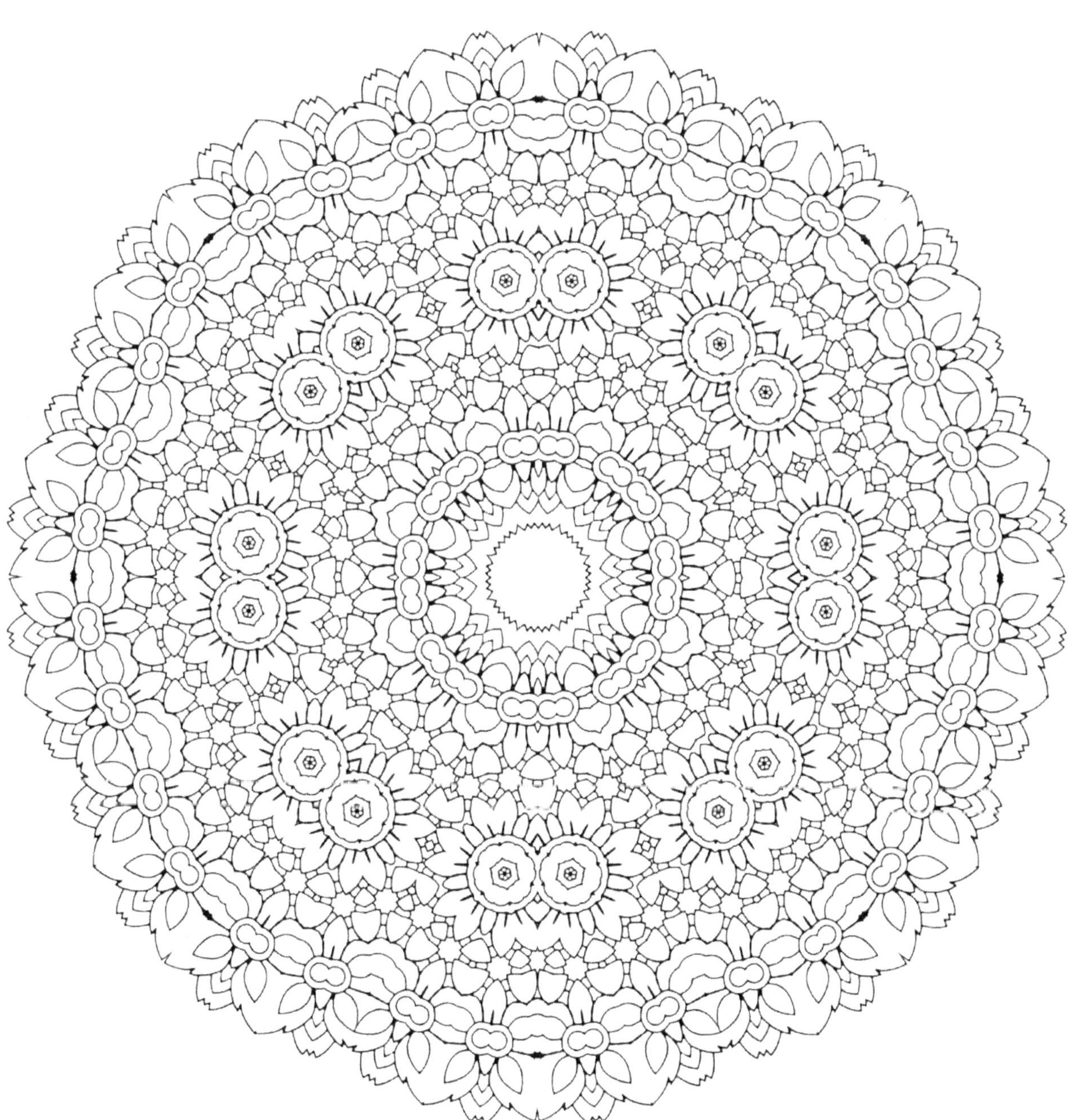

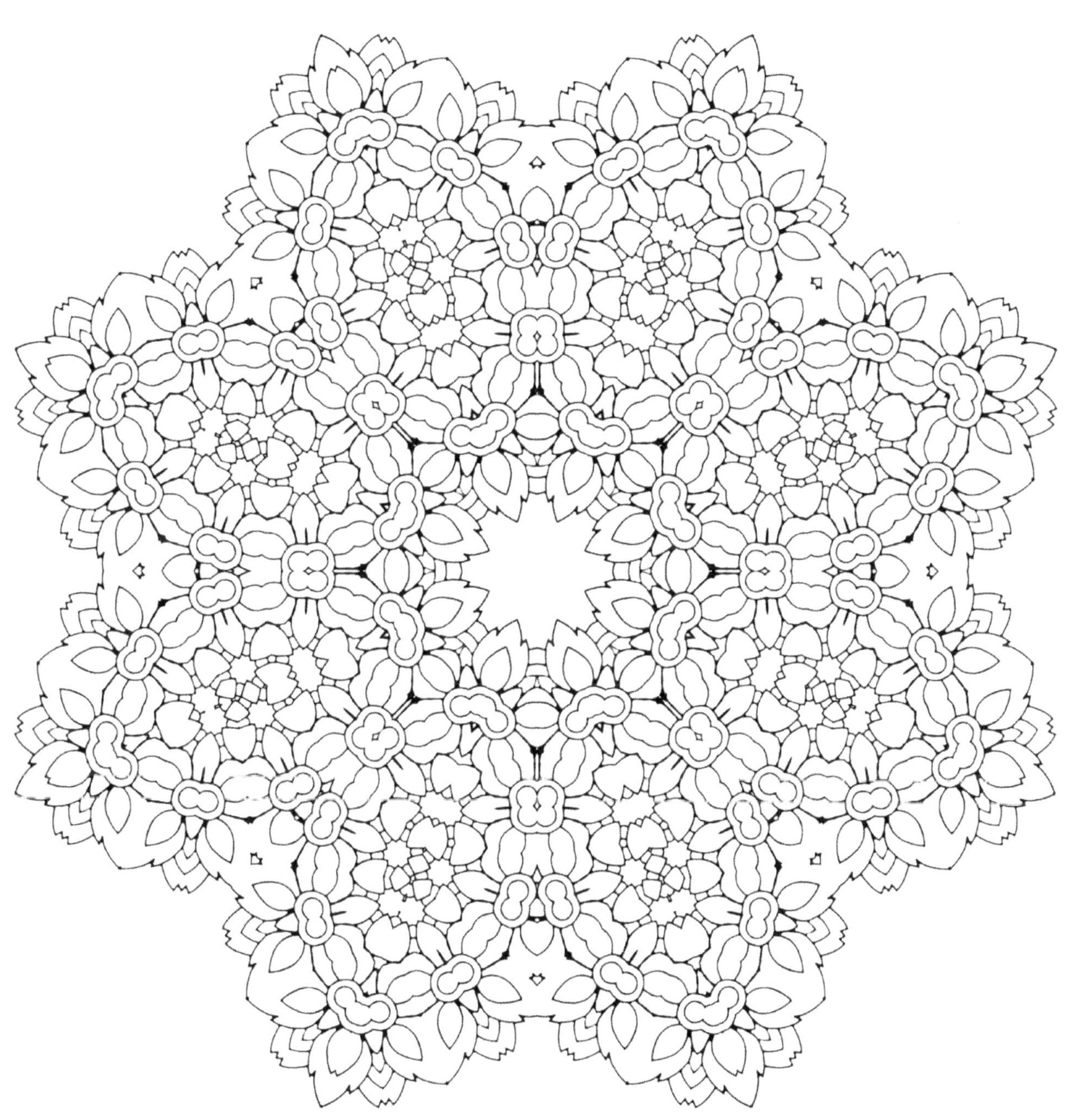

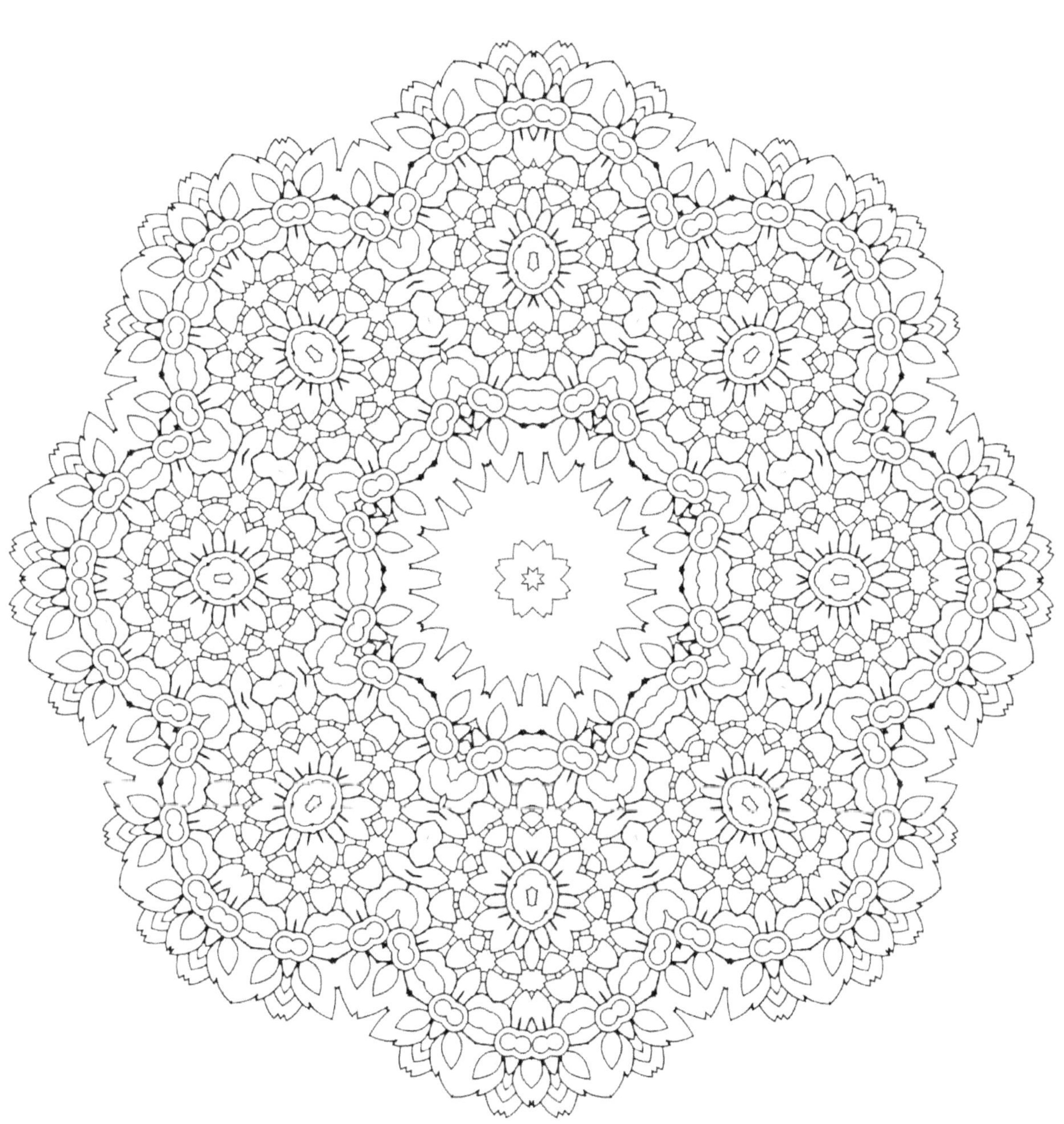

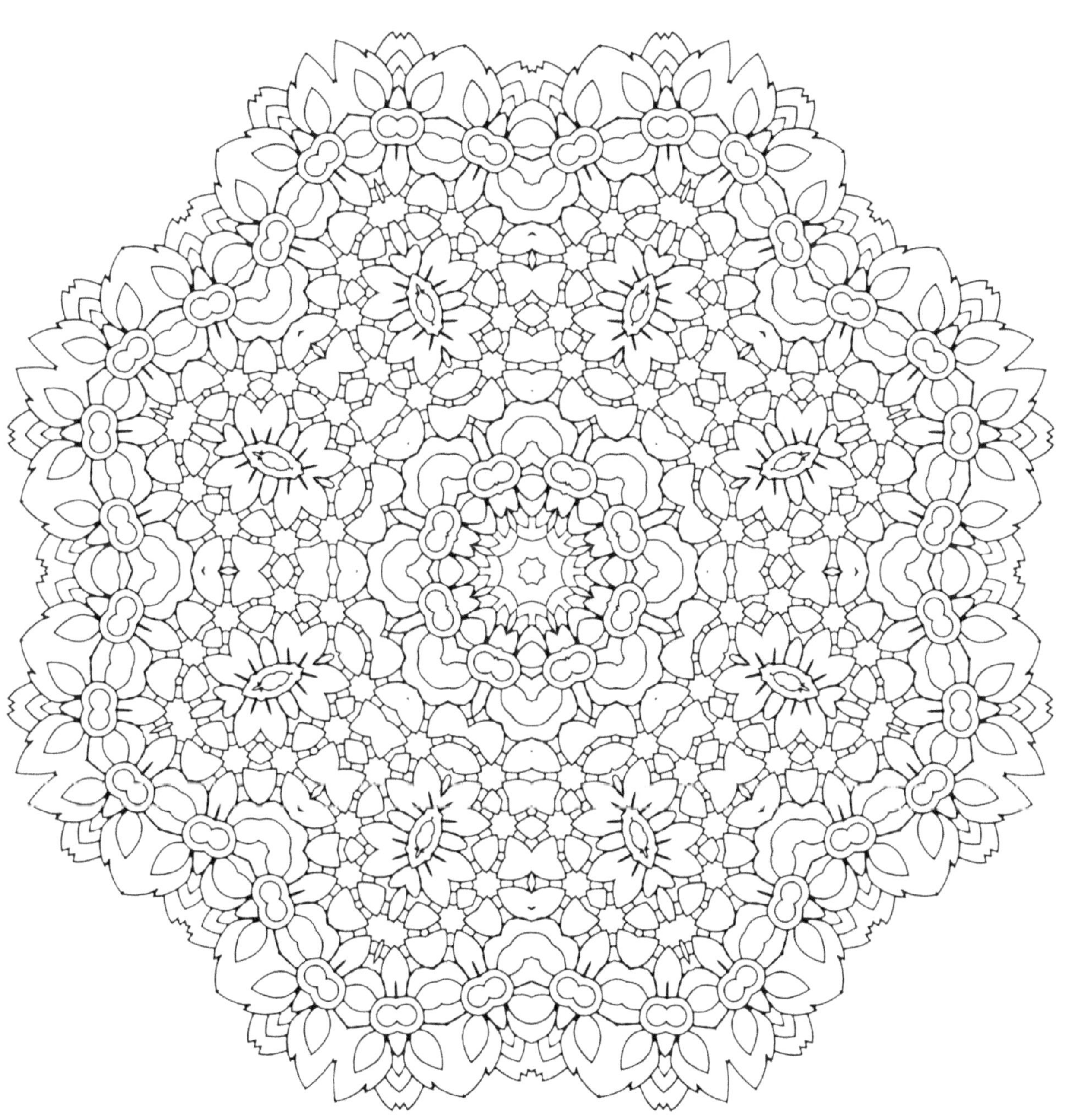

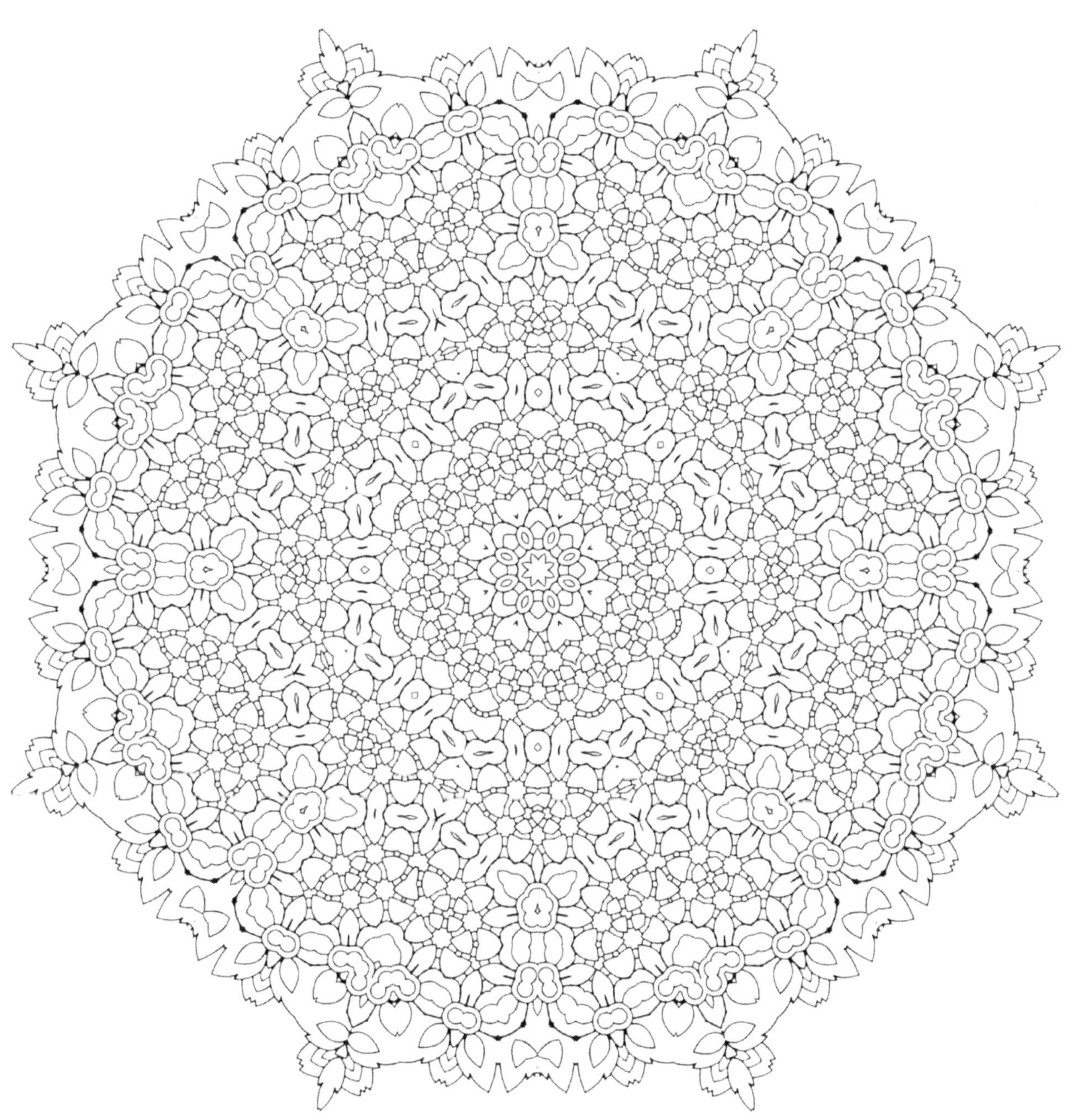

Thank you